# ENTER MOON

**Laura Blomvall** is a Finnish poet living in Bristol. *Enter Moon* is her first pamphlet.

© 2025, Laura Blomvall All rights reserved; no part of this book may be reproduced by any means without the publisher's permission.

ISBN: 978-1-917617-33-8

The author has asserted their right to be identified as the author of this Work in accordance with the Copyright, Designs and Patents Act 1988

Cover designed by Aaron Kent

Edited and Typeset by Aaron Kent

Broken Sleep Books Ltd
PO BOX 102
Llandysul
SA44 9BG

# Contents

| | |
|---|---|
| WHEN STATUES BREATHE | 7 |
| TAMMIKUU / JANUARY | 8 |
| ENTER MOON, THE MYSTIC | 9 |
| THE BIRDS HAIKU | 12 |
| HITCHCOCK'S VERTIGO | 13 |
| LÄNSIRANNIKKO / WEST COAST | 15 |
| FIVE VENUS SONNETS | 16 |
|     ANADYOMENE | |
|     NEBULOSITY; OR MARS TEACHES PIANO TO NERIO | |
|     HOUSEBOUND | |
|     VENUS UNCHAINED | |
|     VICTRIX | |
| ROMAN HOLIDAY HAIKU | 21 |
| KIN | 22 |
| BARBENHEIMER | 23 |
| SINCE RUNNING UP THAT HILL | 24 |
| LEPPÄLINNUT / REDSTARTS | 26 |
| DIPTYCH FOR DENIS VILLENEUVE | 27 |
|     BIBI'S BAR. NIGHT | |
|     STILLTENT. SUNRISE | |
| THE MEG HAIKU | 31 |
| WINTER SWIMMING | 32 |
| THREE POEMS FROM THE WINTER WAR | 37 |
|     RED ICE | |
|     SPECTRES | |
|     THE EAST IS ON FIRE | |
| | |
| ACKNOWLEDGEMENTS | 43 |
| NOTES | 44 |

# Enter Moon
---
## Laura Blomvall

Broken Sleep Books

# WHEN STATUES BREATHE

*LEONTES*

>Would you not deem it breathed?

*PAULINA*

I don't know if you can tell how the air
feels when flesh has stilled to stone. The sun spreads
through the colonnade with some colour, not
too much of it. Look, up – shore larks migrating
to flatlands for winter, this air metes time –
it brushes fingers away, again, away –
nothing that keeps sinking remains. She exhales
rhythms that fly by forgetting the shipwrecks,
feathers that stretch elastic bands. Names, harvests,
peerage of branches, it all leaves her. All
is lurch from here.

*HER*

>My heart's passerine – filed

arrows arranged for perching on his trees.

| TAMMIKUU | JANUARY |
|---|---|

Taivas ilmestyy
niin kirkkaasti kuin vodka
puhtaasta lasista.

January sky
appears as clear as vodka
through a washed glass.

# ENTER MOON, THE MYSTIC

**ENTER**

She's hoarding hope in her halo, vertical

with want when summer dusk leans off to sleep.

One cloud a mask, another a wedding veil.

*To keep you safe*, Cloud whispers, climbing upwards,

wind lifting her skirt. Togetherness seeking

shade under olive trees by the dry stream.

o

Flies scour the air with wings, carving a bowl

to measure heat, its hermitage. His horse's

organs dried without knowing resurrection.

Only hurt of human speed — how it pollutes

leaves. Moon alone seeks soliloquy in trees.

Tonight, there'll be his blood to warm her cheeks:

**MOON**

« I'm allowed to harvest my desire. Then
what, if I have at him? I wrap his hairs
around my rays, my nail-feathered curves grazing
his neck, clean gauze over wound. *Beat on
that thick cloud of unknowing with a sharp
dart of longing love.* Weep for my loneliness
in heaven's necrosis, trapped in the orbits
of Gravity's reins and neighs. How he rules
and rules, old dictator, dragging his heels
through Galaxy's dim stage. There is no
escaping him, his age or closing door.
I gather men's bodies with the last rites
of my tides. With lack I mirror their sick
hearts and veins, kiss eyes closed sans tongue to lick
the stamps. *Here, here.* What's Afterlife's new address —
now Earth's far fallen, where to send their gaze.
I want to find ways to say what I need.
A spider's leg that weaves new corners in
Ophiuchus, who hides the sins that froth
from the Earth's tilt backwards. *I'll say.* I'd like
to stare at his eyes forever, but I know
they'll be missed at my feet. *¡I'll say!* Let me
send them to Starlight, scatter hope in shape

of a hoof, corpse-rouge on my brother Sun's
cheeks. As full as him I'll lie down this time, gripping
wrists of Darkness, my bedpost, my vow, halo's
edge where I conjure no-mores with a *Hello.* »


## , THE MYSTIC

*It must always be in this cloud, this darkness;*
*only by love he can be grasped and held.*
When the end of the world blooms in hearts
and children's veins have eroded to air,
Virgo's work of egg sacs begins to hatch
within Night's folds. Universe is cold sweat
in Moon's sheets, a creased pillowcase of planets'
jasmine. 'I'm not so afar I won't catch
the illness of airborne light. From the stars
I shiver — height being my lung.' She casts
long shadows, an ossuary, an eclipse
of *before* and *after* in the clock's hands.

## THE BIRDS HAIKU

The phone rings inside

glass — to be buried alive

in feathers of birds.

## HITCHCOCK'S VERTIGO


There she died, where redwood trees took no notice:
her hair spreads strays of blonde in Fort Point Bay.

They drive to her suicide scenes and kiss,
her dress sinking downstream with the bouquet.

*Did you have dreams, Madeleine, of what his*
*shipyard would mean before you scaled the stairway?*

Her shadow slips into his hug, an abyss
of deadly leaps that scratch noon's backlit runway.

San Francisco waves pull away what's amiss
in her life. That wasn't part of the play.


                      Her heels ascend in shadows, the stairs' spiral.
                          *Johnny-O, Johnny-O. Will you go on?*

                          Inside a hospital, he visits final
                cuts of her soaked blonde hair, a rope to atone.

'Pain is only palpable, not arrival',

they explain and add that when he is alone

seeing ladders turns his mind centrifugal.

*Fold away maps, they won't show where I've gone;*

*I gathered dahlias, a sense of normal.*

His mind lowers in shadows. The stairs spiral.

## LÄNSIRANNIKKO

## WEST COAST

Auringonlasku,
tulenkynsi, raapii yön
nilkkaa tuhkaksi.

Sunset, a finger-
nail of fire scratches at
night's ashen ankles.

# FIVE VENUS SONNETS

## 1. ANADYOMENE

Ionian Sea revolves over rocks,
currents curl beneath a labouring surface.
She emerges, pearl-eyed, from foam — her face
Erycine clay in sky's hands, thrown by shocks
of sand in ebbing tides when beaches open
to receive libations poured from Uranus.
His blood's exhausted in the birth of Furies.
The first patriarch's sunk down with the sun.

In the beginning of all love, she, fallen
bearer of light, climbs out of white-blue waves
that collapse over her head, bathed by grave
depths and the sun, a web of beams hauling
the catch of her hair from the sea. She will
stray with him, until the last waves tune still.

## 2. NEBULOSITY; OR MARS TEACHES PIANO TO NERIO

You play her skin like those piano keys.

Nuvole Bianche shade, your hand glides

across the flat rain tones, pacing the inside

and outside of a note with tender ease.

TV sound — *Come fai sbagli?* — lingers

in the air — the flag of the quaver dips

on the sheet — beneath the stave, the head slips

down the line, touched — (lightly) — with your ring finger.


Quiddru ca ulìa, sulu se uei.

This sheet of music clouding minds with night

shining, minor harmonies floating away.

She talks in tune with your measured tremolo.

End of a chord, so many keys of white:

cumulus and tense, a loosening echo.

## 3. HOUSEBOUND

From the desert, sirocco sweeps in gusts
of sand, fistfuls of draught, to silt the nerves —
it enters our mouths, sleeves of shirts, it swerves
to lift Sicilian skirts we cannot adjust
down. No gates will close: the gods' breath will comb
the hills for openings like it's a game
between men. Push the door against the frame,
with more force, without end. The air will storm

inside hills like a fever while I sit
down on his chair, listless, waiting for sand
to enter gaps in walls, the damage expand.
In his hands, he holds mountains, hoards counterfeit
coins, a hammer's throat. There's nowhere to go;
only follow with eyes where winds will blow.

## 4. VENUS UNCHAINED

The heated heights of devout want, the need
to be together without faith and allow
his god-like heart to be compelled to vow
to bind us in his nets until we bleed.
The fire that rekindles from the ashes
of his unyielding promises and remorse;
the forgiveness overcoming the force
of the daily chains our creed unleashes.

Hold me, hold me, before his second coming
to this reign of sulphurous and stifling hell,
where crusts of skin melt, belts crack, hills open
in an entangled scream, a muffled moan.
Let us cling to the cross, to Christ's suffering.
Let us breathe pure air through his collapsed lungs.

## 5 VICTRIX

Because Christ was crucified and his hands

nailed like hinges, fitted to hold out air.

Because he yielded his last breath to spare

us from dying, saying how he understands.

Because when he sealed the world with his love,

no mistake, missed turning became too great

for him not to heal; and whatever strait

divorced us, he will shield us with his raft.


And because my time with you was his gift,

I will pledge myself to repairing future;

knowing one day my soul will be with you,

fixed by your side in a world where all grief

and all memories fade: where nightmares I

still touch are lost in endless light spreading.

## ROMAN HOLIDAY HAIKU

Her head in profile,

sleeping in relief — a coin

cast in a fountain.

# KIN
*For Julia*


She turns on the lights in Belvedere Villa.
Her practiced hand has allotted beds, the spray
that holds at bay the wings in walls. Her joy
from our joy is the sun bestowing warmth
in the pool's blue for Harry to cool in;
a hare leaping away from Fiat headlights.
Joan's prepared a banquet, Dan drives us back.
Suzannah's fizzing, Charlotte mixes spritzes.

The way dusk spares its haze over Umbria's
hills, she unwraps olives and gifts of care,
a call in the villa's stones. We're her friends,
fireflies that sway to Swift and spells sifted
from flames: Babel, ancientness, kin, proximal,
explicitly, instead. She's stoking hearths.

## BARBENHEIMER

Imagine clouds at sunset —
orange, hot fuchsia —
a powder rounded with fire.

Directions in pink: *alarmed*,
*press here*, *radiant*.
Smiles painted on surfaces,

her core charged on conveyor
belts of want, waiting
for girls' arms' reach to expand.

'You're a bomb, Barbie.' ('Thanks, Ken!')
'Boom, boom, so much fun.
Let's fill your tank, light you up.'

Curves perfect, atomic; waist
un-elastic. Step
forward, soles arching in air.

## SINCE RUNNING UP THAT HILL

Darling, listen to the stopwatch, starting
gun in the wind weathermen call beast.
It doesn't hurt me. You want to feel
how it feels, hear the deal that I'm making?

Let me give birth without fault lines, without
buildings sliding in the sinking ground.
I slip down on my back without turning.
Let me lie still, my spine like stalactite.

If I could, I'd make a deal with God
to change places with the earth's stripped surface.
Where I end, I will have heartbeats race,
nerves of seeds, roots, that move me like traffic.

*Hear this prayer. It's not yet too late*
*to convert time, with God on side ready*
*to swap our places. He's here now, waiting,*
*on the vanishing top of the hill.*

My knees freeze in winds like snow-capped mountains,
it's earth and me that won't be unhappy
since running up that hill, that Everest.

My body still burns with a red light —
come, angel, lift your foot off the gas,
with stairs to climb there's no rush. My lungs
have shut swallowing your thunder, my crossed
legs have left their trace on the wet sand.
If I only could, I'd make this pact:
trap avalanche in my kneecaps, exhaust
in the brushed hemisphere of my hair.

*I pull the trigger, flashbacks from shadows,*
*there's a bullet waiting inside you.*
*I see flight paths. You see a raised hand,*
*fragments of speed that leave us both bleeding.*

When currents slow and your shirt's pulled back,
I meet the sting, anger in your eyes.
You think I spurn you when I say 'stop',
but I'm only here to turn back time,
shift years, sift the bullets in my bowl
like gold rush in Yukon, hands in water.

*Hear my prayer. The pain I ask for*
*is already near. God is here now,*
*on the vanishing top of the hill.*

| LEPPÄLINNUT | REDSTARTS |
|---|---|

| | |
|---|---|
| Auringonpyörä | The wheel of sunlight |
| sytyttää lehdet, ajaa | ignites the green leaves and drives |
| linnut pesistään. | redstarts from their nests. |

# DIPTYCH FOR DENIS VILLENEUVE

## BIBI'S BAR. NIGHT.
*After Doxie #2 in Blade Runner 2049 (2017).*

'Wanna buy a lady her next cigarette?"

To lean against the door, idle in rain,

is to advertise a service: a chance

to be in sync, off-worldly repertoire

of love, his *I* to her firewalled *Thou*.

The three of them glitch in towering heels

towards his trench coat, soaked with noir, crowd

him, — 'Hi', 'Hello, A-boy, all alone?', — brush

his epaulette. Nails pressed against clear Perspex,

they find him past neon signs, pixelated

feet en pointe to Tchaikovsky, hyperreal in

thin film of rain.

                      The clouds beat the streets blue

with their drained archive, ones and zeros empty

their inner screens. From any entry sign —

even a drop of lack touching an eardrum —

eyes flicker. *To save thee.* And so on. Or,

*I would fain know herself from the blame of*

*all my dreams.* ('Slot a new coin in the machine'.)

The agent shades her eyes from shame of storms.
*We're all here to learn how to control light,*
*how to shift it in columns* – 'the man wearing
the green jacket', she says. 'The one who killed
Sapper. Find out what he knows.' Doxie #2's
eyelashes motion left and right, umbrella's
ribs wind-bent sideways. 'Jätkä on blade runner.
Se on vitun vaarallinen.' Like black
tires splashing water from the full gutters
of an open heart, her pursed mouth, her Finno-
Ugric rubrics U-turn frail, futuristic.
He could un-strike her match, had he at hand
her flame.

    HOT / ГОРЯЧИЙ dissolve in odd
angles of rain. They move the dark with letters.

## STILLTENT. SUNRISE.
*Lady Jessica to herself, then to her son, Paul Atreides. After Dune (2021).*

If you've ever had a moment of sinking

on the ground on your knees, you know there's no

such grain of now. Grief's mornings aren't like sand.

They stretch, air depositing draught, leave-taking

corrosive mounds until the angled edge

sinks under its own hand, birthing the ridge

of a dune. On your palms in the sand, leeward

side of winds.

                    It's said the planet felt little

of our sinking in his gravity, reaping

sediments of old losses in his fist.

To him, it's same as forms of lifting; pockets

of evening primrose or camel sage. Sweat

and tears return untethered to your tongue

from the stilltent fabric — moon after moon,

memory of water caught in the *O*

underneath the dune, the *U* of the ear

of Muad'Dib searching roots of creosote

bush for seeds. *Ou – O·u – Oh you* — the vowels

of the desert.

                    Holding his weeping eye,

how he bends in the expanding diaphragm

of your arms. House of Atreides' son taxed
in sign language of sand is where you sink.
Here, arid tears — no torniquets to save
blood pouring from the hourglass. His dreams
the palmistry of winds, a worm-tooth blade,
your son surrenders agency to sand.

I land on my hands in dust from your Voice.
I know there's no solid ground when eroded
rock wears off flesh from bone. Now I sink down
on my knees, make study of when to mourn.
*There will be nothing. Only I will remain.*
'You know who you are. You know who you are.'

## THE MEG HAIKU

After catacombs

exhumed from cold, a choir

of bite marks on glass.

## WINTER SWIMMING
*For Jenni*


**1.**

I don't descend all the way the first time,

only the second. A fractal fugue gluing

cruise ships to South Harbour, thin ice wraps

across the bay, adhering dreams of reaching

Tallinn, Stockholm or Mariehamn. I listen

to the cold's ghostly half breves: dry flakes

hurling in Eastern winds like gods' hair,

the origin of Finnish song flurrying

from psalteries, dust of pike's jawbone.

It's minus eight degrees, November. Εὖρος,

or here say: östliga vindar / itä-

tuulet / восточные ветры.


**2.**

                        Wind-pierced,

lungs sing through the ribs like two wings

tracking biometric gales, their nomadic

notes printed in intracranial keys.

First time, I follow my body's loudness.

*Through her skin, it is much safer in – instincts*

*tell me to keep breathing in, out, in, out.*

Second, I listen to the stillness beneath —

stripped to my bikini, I step in water,

melt in the grey paints of the glacial sea.

If you still your mind, ice will embrace you,

beguile you with its bold adrenaline,

its moon-holed reasoning. The way you would

use your left foot to hold down Cristofori's

pedal.

    The worst part is when the waves reach

my hardened nipples, touch the sharper quavers

of my collarbones. I try not to gasp.

I've gone down too slow — my legs have gone numb.

I push myself in the sea's fin-of-eel

ebb, take four, five strokes from the iced steel ladder,

its scales-towards-depths. Then turn back. Enough.


**3.**

This morning, Jenni warned me, handing over

porridge: *Beginners shouldn't stay in longer*

*than two minutes. And bring a warmer hat.*

She lives in Helsinki with James, her boyfriend

from Hampshire. We met in London; she wrote

on Virginia Woolf, mermaids, sisters, birds.
They left after Brexit, wild swam each morning
during the pandemic. I moved to Bristol,
sounding foreign in my own mother tongue.
(*Not from here?* the barman quipped last night,
which stung me. I offered to show him my passport.
Jenni sat in the corner, grinning: *He's
interested in you.*) Clouds of crowd-breath haze
the triple-glazed bar windows. Labels peel
off chilled bottles, unglued by condensation,
shivering off our beers' algae-brown glass.


**4.**

The men coming out of the sea grunt, puff
out their chests. Having conquered their bodies
in swim shorts, they walk off, their thighs spread wide.
The women are silent, gaze at the ground,
like merging with the cold to them is yet
another display of sleight of hand; wiping
of fingerprints after pilgrimage, more
ora et labora. Alone, I post
a photo on Instagram, apply filters
on the scene, closed source shimmer from Metaverse.

My English friends, Sam, Julianne and Ben,

reply with cold face and clapping emojis.

My then lover, Scott, from Forest of Dean,

texts how he waited for more nudity.

Not just the bleakness of the Baltic Sea

with its white horizon, its chiselled stave.

**5.**

In the sauna, senses return to you,

heat clasps your skin in a deadly hug.

A ciborium, kiulu cradles water

from the shower taps in its pine-carved prayer.

There are all sorts of bodies — we all mutate

into different shapes sitting up or curling

into ourselves, welcoming the hot steam.

Flat chests, breasts stretched from breastfeeding.

Shaved bodies, bodies with natural hair.

Our skins are as vagrant as the sea: smooth,

wind-rippled, warmed by sunlight, frozen, alive.

*I don't want the new nuclear plant... I'm worried*

*for my father, he forgets things... a release*

*from Russian gas... my memories trip me...*

*throw in some more water* — and water hisses

on the stones, löyly rising to the ceiling,

holding all women's words, hot sibilants

blowing kisses up our calves. Call and response

of shared keys, a downward economy

of exhalation. I cover my mouth

with my hands, it's easier to breathe that way.

The air inside my locked fingers feels cool.

My palms loosen, belonging to this heat.

# THREE POEMS FROM THE WINTER WAR

## RED ICE
*After Yrjö Jylhä, "Kaivo" (1941)*

The sun rises with cannon fire, some shelling.
We hear no charge to advance from our dugout.
Light ricochets off the flurrying shrapnel.


A quiet whisper: 'Please bring me some water.'
He is hot to touch, his pulse beating faster.


By midday, the air shimmers scythe-grey, clouds
of bullets circle the path to the well.
Red ice has wreathed an O around its lips.
Wounded can't ask for water; nor the ill.
The men chew on black snow, if they can find
drifts unspoiled by smoke or urine or shrapnel.
They wait for dark to render Russians blind.


A quiet whisper: 'Please bring me some water.'


One man grabs the jug, picking up the voice
of his friend weak with fever. He sprints over
the upturned earth not noticing the noise

of cannons or guns. He fades in the whir
of metal, the boom of iron. The sky
above's a mess of smoke and snow, shelled trees.
Time stills. He could be lost, or gone much further.

He is hot to touch, his pulse beating faster.

Night falls. "There's a man, his mouth over the well",
they say, "his veins are draining in the water."
There's nothing left to drink – no one can quell
their thirst with blood seeping into the mortar.
The clots and drops have iced to red crystals
and glow like fresh constellations of stars.

He is hot to touch, his pulse beating faster.
A quiet whisper: 'Please bring me some water.'

## SPECTRES
*After Yrjö Jylhä, "Aavepartiot" (1941)*

They watch the roads like spectres in the night,
view forces crossing from the East increase.
New numbers, fresh targets. Covered in white
garments, they glide over ice on their skis
strapped to their heels in skill-drilling winds.
These wingèd wraiths could be anywhere,
their trails blown away by quickening air.


In night's light, they cast no visible shadow,
cold-skinned ghosts never charged to be at ease
create no prints to track in drifting snow.
With only a soul, or two, left with skis
to hunt away invading enemies
new bodies arise from the frozen earth
to unnerve with their terrible rebirth


the ermine moon: they have burrowed for years
the Finnish wilderness, for centuries
carrying their rifles and axes and spears.
An army of phantom patrols on skis
have soared to the border, robbed of its peace.
They bring a white death, unseen — here — *then there* —
their trails blown away by quickening air.

## THE EAST IS ON FIRE
*After Yrjö Jylhä, "Idässä Palaa" (1941)*

The East is on fire. Smoke covers our fields.

Bells ring in alarm and farm windows shake.

A black film clings to our streets, trees and lakes,

holding us quiet in horror, as the winds

roll from the border, bringing noxious fumes

that swirl around the barns and fresh-cut sheaves.

A single finch dares sing under the eaves

shielded from the sun's rays, ruffling her plumes.

Flames stretch their wingspan, fusing with daylight.

We've delayed our work in an unplanned rest

to scan the fire aflight from the roadside.


The East clears. The wind carries the smoke west,

revealing Karelia. With her bright

scalpel, the moon wounds the ash-faced forest.

## ACKNOWLEDGEMENTS

I am grateful to Denise Saul, W.N. Herbert, Rebecca Tamás, Chad M. Crabtree and Carrie Etter for selecting poems from this pamphlet for publication in *The Poetry Review, Propel Magazine, Arboreal Magazine* and *Zócalo Public Square*.

Thank you to Anni Pal for permission to publish the Yrjö Jylhä translations, and for her comments on early versions of 'Three Poems from the Winter War'.

Special thanks to Penny Boxall, Lucy Cheseldine, James Coghill, Rowan Evans, Sophie Hall-Luke, Robin Morton, Matthew Neale, Catherine Olver, Phoebe Power and Jenni Råback for suggestions on versions of some of these poems; and most especially to Suzannah V. Evans for being the first person to read through the full manuscript and for her generous edits and ongoing encouragement.

My gratitude to Aaron Kent and the Broken Sleep family for giving this pamphlet such a welcoming home.

## NOTES

WHEN STATUES BREATHE. 'Would you not deem it breathed', from William Shakespeare, *The Winter's Tale*.

ENTER MOON, THE MYSTIC. 'Enter Moon' and 'Tonight, there'll be his blood to warm her cheeks', after Ted Hughes's translation of Federico García Lorca, *Blood Wedding*. *'It must always be in this cloud, this darkness; only by love he can be grasped and held'* from *The Cloud of Unknowing*. The poem first appeared in *Propel Magazine*.

2 NEBULOSITY; OR MARS TEACHES PIANO TO NERIO. 'Quiddru ca ulìa…sulu se uei' after Ludovico Einaudi, 'Nuvole Bianche'.

KIN. 'Babel, ancientness, kin, proximal, explicitly, instead', from Joan Passey, *Cornish Gothic, 1830-1913*.

SINCE RUNNING UP THAT HILL. The poem was inspired by and borrows from the Kate Bush song, 'Running Up That Hill (A Deal With God)'. The poem first appeared in *Zócalo Public Square*.

BIBI'S BAR. NIGHT first appeared in *Arboreal Magazine*.

WINTER SWIMMING. *'Through her skin, it is much safer in – instincts / tell me to keep breathing in, out, in, out'* from Kate Bush, 'Breathing'. The poem first appeared in *The Poetry Review*.

THREE POEMS FROM THE WINTER WAR. The original Finnish poems were published in Yrjö Jylhä, *Kiirastuli.*

# LAY OUT YOUR UNREST

www.ingramcontent.com/pod-product-compliance
Lightning Source LLC
LaVergne TN
LVHW041310080426
835510LV00009B/947